VIKING
LIST BUILDING

FREE AXE
SWINGING
LESSON
put your email
BELOW ↓

Chapter 1:

Create or Acquire

Overview

Welcome to Viking List Building! This is a special list building strategy designed to accomplish two things: 1) get a list building apparatus set up within one hour and 2) achieve high opt-in rates.

This strategy basically revolves around leveraging the appeal of video courses to generate opt-ins.

Why Video Courses?

People have developed "banner blindness" when it comes to eBooks, Free Reports, PDFs, that sort of thing. It still works, especially if you have the time and money to invest in making large, spectacular looking, high quality eBooks and reports, but even then, it just doesn't convert quite as well any more.

However, when we've sent traffic to opt in pages where we were offering free access to video courses, we saw opt in rates as high as 78%! This is particularly effective when you apply a special visual theme or mascot to your lead magnet as opposed to a generic name with a generic image, but we'll get to that in lesson 2.

We're going to show you how you can make a Viking List Building machine just like that in less than an hour. So, without further ado let's have a look at this course.

Chapter 1 deals with video content options. This is where we'll discuss how to either make or acquire video content to use as a lead magnet. Don't worry, you'll be surprised how quick and easy this is.

Chapter 2 shows you how to make a gorgeous 3d eCover graphic of your video content for your squeeze page.

Chapter 3 walks you through how to quickly and easily design a simple, minimalist squeeze page geared towards maximizing conversions.

Chapter 4 covers various free and paid traffic methods and finally your battle plan for implementing what you've learned.

Remember, this can all be done within 1 hour. So, if you're ready, let's dive in to Chapter One.

Create or Acquire

So, for creating the video lesson or course you're going to be using as a lead magnet or a free gift, you basically have 2 choices: Create it yourself or Pay for it.

Let's look at the first option. Creating video content is beneficial because it can be done for free and somewhat quickly, though not as quickly as buying pre-made content. Now there's basically three types of video creation options:

• Talking head

• Slide presentation

• Screen cast

Let's look at the talking head option:

Now many of you might immediately become a little anxious or worried about this option if you haven't done this before so let's put the worry to rest. Go online, go to YouTube and type in violin lessons. What you'll see is a bunch of people staring at their web cams or maybe their smart phone cameras with a fiddle in their hands talking about the basics of violin playing and maybe scratching out a tune or two. Now does that look expensive? Nope. Does it look complicated? Definitely not (well unless of course you don't know how to play a fiddle). But the point is you can create any sort of "talking head" lesson that you have experience in with nothing more than yourself and your web cam or smart phone.

But what about those of you who have stage fright and wouldn't be caught dead getting in front of a camera? Well for you guys let's move on to the next option: Slide presentations.

For the Slide presentation approach, you'd basically draft up an outline of your lesson and prepare it in bullet format via any slide presentation software like PowerPoint. Then you'd audio record your presentation either with your computer or your smartphone or any other device you prefer. Finally, you'd take that audio file and sync it with your slide presentation. Now the most common slideshow software, PowerPoint, actually has a function for exporting your presentation to a video file and if you search YouTube you'll see there are plenty of easy video tutorials on how to do it. And oh by the way, you'll notice those tutorials are actually recordings of a person's computer screen while he or she walks you through the process which, incidentally, brings us to the last option: the screen cast.

The screen cast is our preferred method because it requires little preparation and can be done in an off the cuff manner. Now although we said creating your video was free, the screencast method will usually require you to invest anywhere from $15 to $50 for screen capture software. That said, it's always worth seeing if you can find any free offers. But let there be no question, a small investment in screencast software will pay off quickly. Basically, all you'll do here is record your screen and your voice while you go through and teach how to do something on the computer. For examples of this you could go to YouTube and search for something like "WordPress tutorial"...

Okay now let's have a look at the second video content choice: acquisition, or paid video content.

There are basically two ways to do this: buying pre-made PLR videos or paying an actor.

PLR stands for Private Label Rights and basically means you can resell these courses usually along with the right to modify, rebrand, or relabel them, and even put yourself down as the author. For buying PLR videos, literally just google "PLR videos" and you'll find plenty of online stores selling cheap PLR video lessons on various topics ranging from web design to cardio workouts. You can usually find these for as little as 4 or 5 bucks ranging all the way up to $20, $50, or even hundreds of dollars. Since we're looking at something to give away for free as a lead magnet, it's alright to stay on the inexpensive side, just make sure the quality itself isn't low.

Your leads will judge you by the quality of the gift you offered them. When you're browsing, don't worry too much about the "look" of the eCover for these PLR videos because once you've bought one, you'll want to rebrand it anyway which will be covered in the next lesson.

Now the other way is to pay an actor to do the video for you. An "actor" can either mean an onscreen "talking head" actor or even just someone who will do a screen cast recording or slide show presentation video for you. Don't worry, the word actor sounds expensive, but there are ways to do this pretty inexpensively such as hiring someone on Fiverr or Upwork or even offering the opportunity to a local college kid or struggling acting student looking to beef up their portfolio.

Whichever method you choose; you'll want to make sure the end product "looks" great. To do this you'll need to design an attractive eCover image which is what we'll cover in the next chapter.

Chapter 2:

eCover Graphics

Welcome to Chapter 2 in which we're going to create eCover graphics for your video lead magnet. Right now let's head inside Myecovermaker.com which is our recommended eCover tool. As you'll see, there are plenty of eCover templates to choose from. Since we're doing a video course, we'll choose a DVD case.

Once we're in the creator, we'll want to choose an image. The first option is to choose an image from myecovermaker.com's library using the "add image" button on the left.

The other option is to click the "upload" button and choose your own image. As you can see we've already got our own image uploaded here. This is something we purchased for a dollar on a stock photo site.

So for this example we'll be pretending we're making a Wordpress training course and that we're going for a pirate theme. Remember, as we mentioned in lesson 1, a special theme or mascot has a greater likelihood of breaking through banner blindness than, say, a generic title like "wordpress for beginners" and a generic image

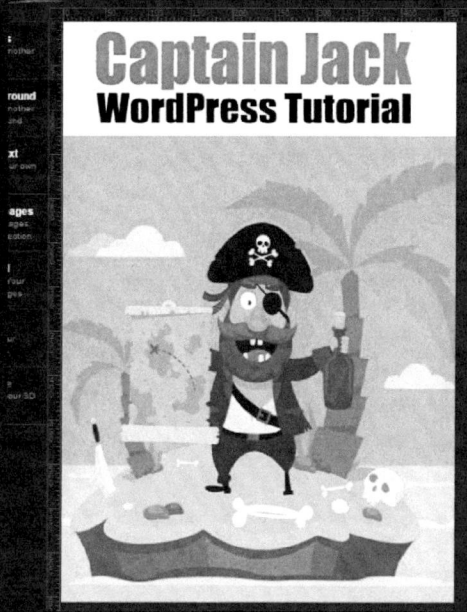

like a photo of a guy at his computer. People see that type of thing all the time and it's not likely to get their attention or look very original. Sure, it's a little cheesy, but the uniqueness pays off in the end.

We'll use the "add text" button to insert a title and sub-title. Let's call this... Captain Jack WordPress Tutorial. In myecovermaker.com you can choose from a multitude of fonts and text effects to make your title pop out.

Adjust your image and text to look however you'd expect a DVD cover to look on the front and, when you're satisfied, click the finalize button. Don't worry, you can always come back and adjust things if necessary.

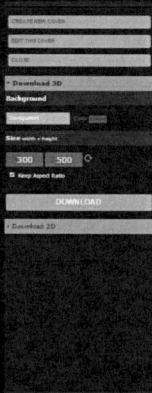

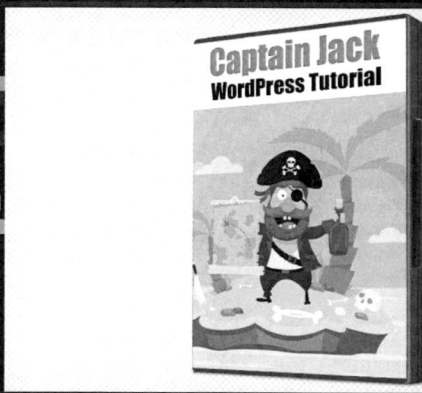

Once your ecover is finalized, be sure to select the transparent background option and click download. When you're satisfied, you can click "close" to return to the dashboard.

Finally, we recommend you use the same image to create an eCover image of an actual disc. Simply click "edit this eCover" which will create a new copy of the one you just made, and inside the editor, click "ecovers" and choose the disc template. You'll have to do some rearranging to make the image and elements look right on the disc but don't worry, the process is just as easy as before.

Next we're going to want to arrange the eCovers into a bundle image. We'll be using creator 7 but you can use any free or paid image editing program you like.

Now we've seen our highest opt in rates when we offer multiple video courses instead of one, so for the sake of this example we've created an additional video course that will be bundled with the original.

We're going to import our transparent eCover files and rearrange them to look presentable. Once you're satisfied with the look, you'll want to export or save the file as a transparent png. In the next lesson we'll be looking at how to incorporate this image into a squeeze page.

Chapter 3:

Squeeze Page Design

Welcome to lesson 3, where we'll be designing your squeeze page. So, for this example we'll using Instapage which is our favorite squeeze page designer, but feel free to use whatever CMS you prefer.

For starters, we're going to choose from one of Instapage's templates. We'll be changing things quite a bit so it doesn't really matter which one we choose.

Now we like to keep things pretty minimalist so the first thing we're going to do is eliminate all the extra rows which can be done by clicking the delete button at the top left of each section.

As for the background, we'll go with plain white for this example which can be done by clicking settings – background – background color – and be sure to remove any background image that's there already.

Next, we'll need to fashion a headline and sub headline. We'll just use the text elements that came with the template. For the headline, let's try "Grab TWO of Our Amazing Video Courses for FREE!" and for the sub headline let's try something like: "Hurry, this FREE offer ends soon. Click the button below to grab your two courses fast!"

Next we'll want to add the eCover bundle image. Just go to "add new" – "image" and upload the image from your computer.

Click "insert" and drag and resize the image to sit just under the sub headline.

Finally, we'll need to add a button. We recommend using the two step opt in strategy as its been shown to have a positive impact on opt in rates. We'll go to "add new" and select "button". Resize the button to your liking and then click "edit".

You'll want to change the button text to a CTA or call to action statement. Many marketers find that using terms from the visitor's perspective like "my" and "me" produce a higher conversion rate. So let's try "Get My Free Courses". Feel free to adjust the style options as you see fit and then click "done"

Next, with the button still selected, we'll click the link icon to bring up the "click event" drop down, and then we'll choose the pop up option.

In this pop up area you'll want to place another headline and an opt in form. Click "headline" and then click "form" too. Arrange the form so it's centered under the headline. For the headline, let's try something like "Tell Us Where to Instantly Send Your FREE Courses".

For the opt in form, the default name and email fields are fine, but you'll want to double-click the button, click on "button style" and enter another CTA. Let's try something like "Send Me My Free Courses!" and click "done".

Next, double click either of the form fields and click on "integrations" from the top menu. This is where you'll choose your auto-responder service and link the opt in form to your desired email list.

When you're finished, click "done" at the top of the page. The second to last step is to click the mobile phone button in the top menu. Here you'll just want to rearrange things to make sure the page looks good on mobile devices. Be sure to click on the button and do the same for the pop up area.

This is typically where you'd click the A/B Split Test button in the top menu if you wanted to do a split test. That's not the focus of this course nor is it a necessity so we're going to skip that step this time but be sure to check out our course on Split Testing if you want to really max out your opt-in rates.

The last step is to make sure your landing page is compliant with legal policies. Typically, you'd see things like a non-SPAM disclaimer and a clear link to a privacy policy so people know they're opting in to a list, but just be sure to look up and follow whatever laws are applicable in your country.

Finally, when you're happy with everything, click "publish" and choose where you want to publish the page. We always just choose the "demo page" option which just means it will be hosted by Instapage.

So now that our page is ready we just need to send some traffic to it, which is what we'll be learning in the next lesson.

Chapter 4:
Traffic Methods

Welcome to Chapter 4 where we'll be discussing methods for driving traffic to your landing page.

Now there's obviously an endless list of free and paid traffic methods but for this course we're going to be focusing on two free methods and one paid method.

Forum Signatures

The first method to consider is the forum signature method. Now this is one of the oldest methods of driving traffic, but it still proves to be an incredibly effective one for marketers to this day.

Basically, you identify a few online forums for your niche, so if you're in the internet marketing niche you'll want to try the warrior forum and if you're in the pet reptiles niche you'll want to check out herp center, and so on.

Create an account at one or more of these forums. Once you've got a profile set up, go to the account settings area of your forum account or maybe the rules section and figure out what the guidelines are for signatures.

A signature is basically a little area that appears at the bottom of each and every single post you make within a forum thread.

Originally this was meant for something similar to an email signature: you'd automatically have your name and contact info, maybe preceded by "kind regards" or something like that, attached to the bottom of your message. These signatures have evolved into more of a self-expression thing. People will often put a famous quote or an image in the signature. As a marketer, you'll want to put a link in there to your squeeze page. Preferably an image that is hyperlinked, but at least a text link.

Now depending on the forum, the rules will be different on how and when you can use a forum signature. Some forums allow you to start using as extravagant a signature as you want right away, others require you to have been a member for a few weeks or to have a certain number of posts or something. Sometimes you can start out with a text only signature and then you're permitted to add an image after you've been around a while. Figure out what the rules are for the forums you join and just start posting. Become part of the community that you intend to market to.

There's one key thing to remember though: don't post so much that it seems you're just spamming to get your links out there. People will notice that right away and you might get suspended or banned.

YouTube Marketing

The other free method to focus on is YouTube marketing. This can be done a few ways. You can either make videos specifically designed to market your free video course or you can make general informational videos about your niche and then mention your free video course as sort of a "go here to learn more" thing. Either way, be sure to put a link to your landing page in your description and consider doing the same as an annotation displayed over the video.

These videos can be webcam videos, talking head videos shot with your smart phone, screen cast videos or slideshow style videos. Generally, the more videos you have and the more useful the content, the more traffic you'll get. Be sure to share your videos on social media as well as to invest some time into typing up an SEO friendly and keyword rich description.

Solo Ads

Now the paid method you may want to consider when you're starting out is solo ads. Solo ad vendors exist for just about every niche out there, but the most common ones are usually ones like the IM niche, the weight loss/fitness niche, and the self-improvement niche. A solo ad vendor is basically someone in one of these niches who has a large list of their own and will send out emails to their list promoting your offer or lead magnet and sending those subscribers to your landing page. You basically charge per click, specifically for each time someone clicks through THEIR link to go to your squeeze page. Some solo ad vendors will allow you to specify the subject line and message, others will insist that they word both of those in a way that their list is used to. The quickest and cheapest way to get your feet wet in solo ads is to join Udimi.com and buy a small volume of clicks from a trusted vendor. They have a review and rating system similar to eBay or Fiverr so you can tell who the serious ones are. However, you want to make sure your leads are high quality and in the world of solo ads, you really do get what you paid for. So, if you're noticing your Udimi derived leads aren't particularly responsive, try doing a search on google or even within the warrior forum for big name independent solo ad vendors. A lot of successful marketers also offer solo ads as a side service and you'll be able to tell which ones produce high quality leads based on the testimonials of other marketers.

Now once you've got your feet wet you should certainly try to branch out into and experiment with other free and paid methods in the realm of social media sharing and pay per click ads. Compare your results with all traffic methods and use whatever works for you.

Battle Plan

Step 1: Record a video or buy a PLR video.

Step 2: Create an eCover.

Step 3: Set up a simple landing page.

Step 4: Start implementing one of these traffic methods.

Don't make the mistake of leaving this eBook without taking action or you probably never will. And definitely don't put it off until you've got everything figured out just perfectly. We both know that means you'll never get started. Start implementing these steps immediately, even imperfectly, and start building your list right now.

9 781648 303739